Mapping
North America

Kate McGough

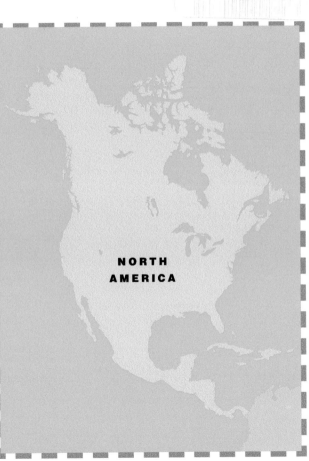

NORTH
AMERICA

North America is one of the seven **continents** in the world. This is what a map of North America looks like.

NORTH AMERICA

③

There are many **lakes** in North America. Lakes look like this on a map.

Find the Great Lakes on the map.

Great Bear Lake

Great Slave Lake

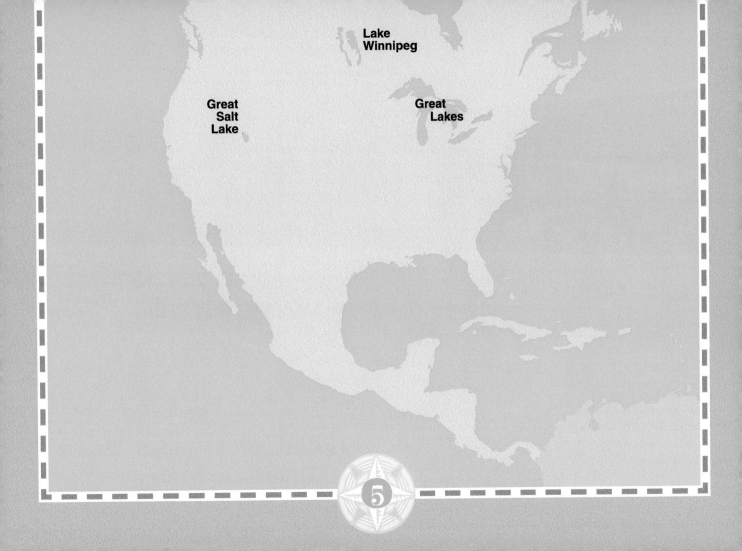

Lake
Winnipeg

Great
Salt
Lake

Great
Lakes

There are many **rivers** in North America.
Rivers look like this on a map.

Find the Yukon River
on the map.

Yukon River

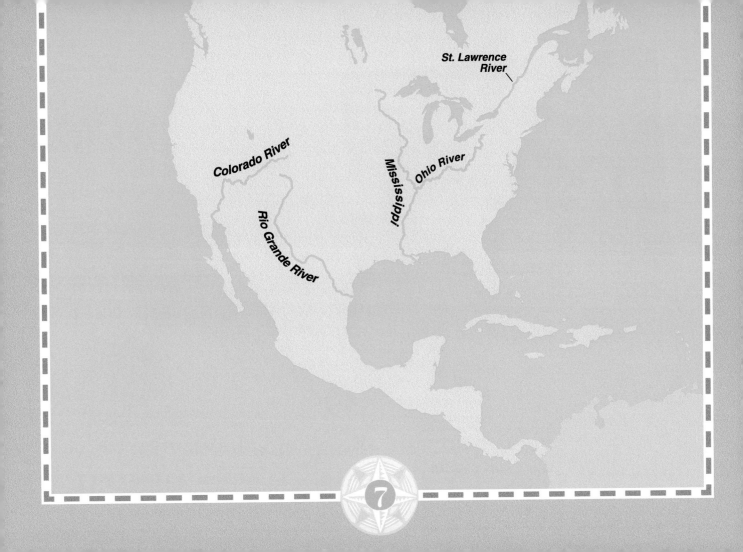

St. Lawrence
River

Colorado River

Ohio River

Mississippi

Rio Grande River

There are many **mountain ranges** in North America.
Mountain ranges look like this on a map.

Find the Rocky Mountains
on the map.

ROCKY MOUNTAINS

APPALACHIAN MOUNTAINS

SIERRA MADRE

There are three **countries** in North America. Country borders look like this on a map.

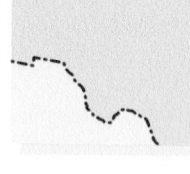

Find Mexico on the map.

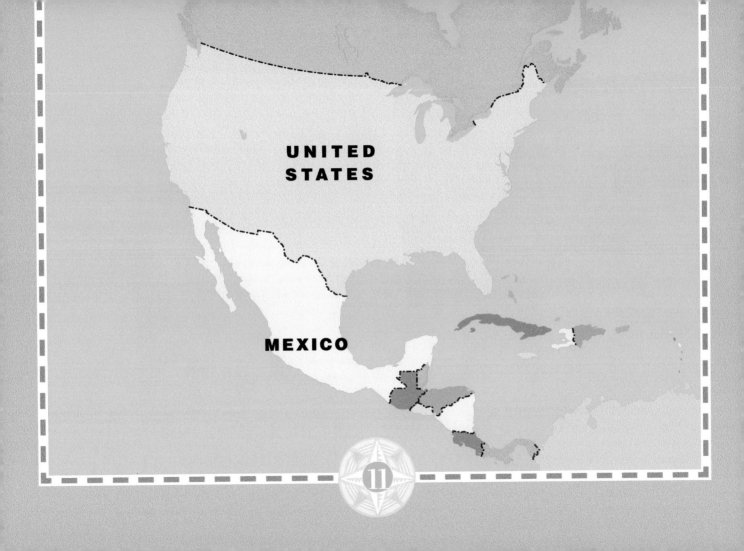

UNITED
STATES

MEXICO

There are many **cities** in North America. Cities look like this on a map.

Find New Orleans on the map.

Vancouver

Ottawa

Chicago

New York

Washington, D.C.

Los Angeles

New
Orleans

Miami

Mexico

13

Great Bear Lake

Great Slave Lake

Yukon River

Look at the map of North America.
Find each of these places:

- ✴ Great Salt Lake
- ✴ Rio Grande River
- ✴ Appalachian Mountains
- ✴ Canada
- ✴ Vancouver

Vancouver

Lake
Winnipeg

*St. Lawrence
River*

MOUNTAINS

Ottawa

Great
Salt
Lake

Great
Lakes

Chicago

New York

UNITED
STATES

Washington, D.C.

Ohio River

Mississippi River

APPALACHIAN MOUNTAINS

Colorado River

Los Angeles

Rio Grande River

SIERRA MADRE

New
Orleans

Miami

MEXICO

Mexico

15

Index

cities	13
continents	3
countries	11
lakes	5
mountain ranges	9
rivers	7